Edmund Clarence Stedman

Octavius Brooks Frothingham and the new Faith

Edmund Clarence Stedman

Octavius Brooks Frothingham and the new Faith

ISBN/EAN: 9783337140977

Printed in Europe, USA, Canada, Australia, Japan

Cover: Foto ©ninafisch / pixelio.de

More available books at **www.hansebooks.com**

O. B. Frothingham

G.P Putnam's Sons. New York.

Octavius Brooks Frothingham

AND

The New Faith

BY

EDMUND C. STEDMAN

NEW YORK

G. P. PUTNAM'S SONS

182 FIFTH AVENUE

1876.

INTRODUCTORY NOTE.

IN response to numerous requests, and to the generally expressed opinion that the material belonged to permanent rather than ephemeral literature, the able essay of Mr. Stedman, which first appeared in "The Galaxy," is here reproduced in book-form.

The growing interest in the purport and influence of what are known as Radical ideas, and the very general recognition of the fact that those ideas have passed through their first and inevitable stage of simple negation and iconoclasm, and are shaping themselves into a positive and constructive faith, and a practical rule of life, form a sufficient ground for the work that the essayist has attempted.

His tèrse yet comprehensive summary of the life and teachings of the man who, more probably than any other American, is the representative and apostle of the liberal faith, will be of interest to all who sympathize with this faith, and of special value to the many whose objections to or dread of Radicalism are founded upon distorted reports and prejudiced impressions.

To Mr. Stedman's effective presentation (which has received the author's revision) has been added an extract from a recent and typical sermon, which gives the teacher's own statement of his faith and life-long purpose.

G. H. P.

OCTAVIUS BROOKS FROTHINGHAM.

IF this philosophical teacher and divine had
chosen to live in some rural spot, or from
an academic grove had sent his thoughts out to
the world—in such case possibly the world's attention would have been more speedily fixed upon
him. He would be even more conspicuous by
position, though not by magnitude, than he has become through his peculiar eminence among the
notable preachers of New York. Settled in a pro-
vincial town, he doubtless would make the place
of his teachings, as Emerson has made Concord, a
modern oracle and shrine.

I.

Frothingham has been called the successor of
Theodore Parker, whose life he has written with equal simplicity, reverence, and
judicial poise. Certainly we have no other man

Parker and
Frothingham.

who, since the death of Parker, has so persistently grounded all religious faith and hope upon the basis of reason, nature, discovered law. No other preacher, taking up the ideas to which Parker finally advanced, has so expanded and developed them in keeping with the steadfast growth of knowledge. The mantle which fell to him rests upon a religious orator who displays less of that magnetic power which, in its lower manifestation, sustains the demagogue, and, in its higher, the noble leader of men; yet upon one who can see to it, by every gift of culture, purpose, and unflagging zeal, that no step is taken backward, and who with his rational intellect has crystallized in a religious system what was at first an inspiration—the revelation of a lofty and impetuous yet somewhat overburdened soul.

Parker stormed traditionalism in its stronghold. Boston, the nucleus of intellectual pride, was so content with the advance of Unitarianism that it was less easy to draw her liberals any further than to disorganize the ranks of the extreme devotees of authority. While Parker

Boston.

was striving to enfranchise religious belief, even a
Roman Catholic was more likely to swing over to
rationalism than was a Unitarian of the period.
Frothingham, the disciple and successor, saw that
to make the work complete he must enter upon a
wider sphere of action. His field must be the world
—the world as represented in a metropolis. Mr.
Conway recently said of London that it afforded
a hearing and companionship to any mind, no matter how eccentric, since there is no person who
will not find among millions, gathered from every
race and country, others of like creed and disposi-

New York.
tion with his own. In New York, since
it has fairly become metropolitan, the
chance to be found is the same as in London, Paris,
and other great cities of the world. Here, then,
Frothingham at least was sure, first, of a foothold ;
secondly, of room for growth ; and hither he came,
to transplant his scion and to nourish it for years.
In such a place as New York enduring qualities are
not those which at once enforce attention. Every
year some new claimant appears in each profession,
and often disappears as quickly. But when posi-

tion is once legitimately attained, it is reputation and power, extending to the borders of the land. Mr. Frothingham at length finds himself not only an authority with his immediate followers, but also, whether he will or no, what is termed a " popular preacher." His church is at the present time one of the widely known resorts of visitors who would acquaint themselves with the characteristic men and places of the city. In making a brief sketch of its leading features we may also touch upon its religious system, and upon the quality and bearing of the preacher to whom it owes a vigorous establishment.

It is believed, that even those readers who are honestly at variance with Frothingham's doctrines *A representative preacher.* must nevertheless take an interest in the power and attitude of the man. No preacher is more fully entitled to the epithet " representative." In temperament and person he is of the purest New England type. As to the former, Edwards, Hopkins, Bellamy, were of the like spiritual, self-contained, and dauntless mold; as to the latter, his form and features repeat characteristics

which have been found among eastern theologians
and scholars from the early colonial times.   He
has the clear-cut face, the intellectual forehead, the
large unarched New England nose, and the pointed
chin—suggesting equally the most delicate refine-
ment and the sturdiest polemical valor.   Here are
the blue-gray, scholarly, half-gentle, half-satirical
eyes, a mobile mouth, compressed and accurate
lips.   The whole head is of the down-east, Brah-
ministic type; somewhat aristocratic,—for the
clergy of the New England colonies were an aris-
tocracy by selection, learning, and faith.   In brief,
here is one whom you might suppose to have
had, like Emerson, eight generations of orthodox
preachers behind him ; a man who, in the light of
an earlier period, might have been a Calvinist of
the sternest order, and have died for his belief, or
have gone out into the forest with as stout a heart
as he brought, in these times, to our " wilderness
of brick and stone."   But we are not living in the
colonial period, and Calvinism, being no longer a
protest, is no longer an instinctive religion with
men of his type and ancestry.

    1*

Let us first convey some notion of the service conducted by him, and then speak of his devotional

Aspiring and progressive spirit. philosophy—remarking that this, while changeless in an essential spirit of aspiration and receptivity, is avowedly subject to modification by whatever knowledge may be acquired. Though its purpose remains the same, its outward form moves in an ascending scale. "More light," is the teacher's perpetual cry, and his belief is ever more freshly and truthfully set forth as new discoveries are apparent to him.

II.

The large hall in the Masonic Temple, at the junction of Twenty-third Street and Sixth Avenue,

Religious service at Masonic Hall. is a place leased on Sundays to Mr. Frothingham's congregation, and devoted to the performance of a religious service. A lofty ceiling rests upon two rows of imposing but somewhat cumbrous pillars, that lead to a semicircular recess and the speaker's chair—above which are visible the ancient symbols of the "craft." Exercises begin at 10 : 45 A. M., but at that time not

more than one-half of the audience has arrived.   It
is an audience of no ordinary kind.   Sincerity and
interest are visible upon the countenances of regular attendants.   A voluntary is performed upon the
organ, and a hymn, possibly selected· from the
Unitarian collection, is sung by a choir of four
voices.   You will not fail to take notice that the
music is exquisite.   This, and the floral decora-
tions of the lecturn, show that here the æsthetic
harmonies are well observed, though rendered subordinate to the main purpose of the hour.   The
preacher rises, and receives close attention.   The
book which he usually reads is one com-

The reading.

piled from the sacred scriptures of many
ancient nations, and entitled "The Sacred Anthol-
ogy;" a work arranged by Moncure D. Conway, in
whose London chapel a liberal service also is held.
Mr. Frothingham begins to read, in tones that at
first are somewhat labored or muffled, but speedily
attract and hold the ear; his voice, despite a few
peculiarities of articulation, having a quality and
distinction of its own.   His chief effort is to convey
the full meaning of the printed text.   "Listen,"

he says, " to the teachings of the ancient scriptures. This is from the Hindu;" or, "This is
from the Chinese;" afterward, " This is from the
Hebrew " (Old Testament); or, "This is from the
Persian ;" or again, " This is from the Christian "
(New Testament); thus giving no precedence in
authority to any selection, but valuing each for its
beauty, wisdom, piety, and internal truth.

After the reading, of this unusual character, the
doors are opened to admit another throng of people, who seat themselves in time for the prayer.
The speaker's voice rises in an invocation
The prayer.
to the Supreme Source of Law and Goodness—an address which is an aspiration, a poem
of reverence, worship, and acknowledgment, but
never, by any chance, a petition to a listening
Ruler for gifts, protection, or other personal and
special benefits. The ties of human brotherhood
are remembered; the noble souls that have sought
for truth in the past, and suffered for it, are spoken
of as the saints whose memory every professor of
the liberal faith must love and cherish, and whose
example it is a holy ambition to imitate. Thus

much of Positivism is often reflected in Mr. Frothingham's speech and prayer. But in assuming for
Religion of Hu- the title of an important volume,* which
manity.
illustrates his religious system, a phrase
adopted by the followers of Comte, he seeks to
invest the beautiful expression with a more expan-
sive and spiritual comprehensiveness. Still, the
idea of human brotherhood, as a religious basis, is
frequently advanced by him in words such as these
—which formed the larger portion of one of his
recent prayers:

"Let us be striving, this morning, to get some nearer
insight into that great Eternity, to which so many things
are passing evermore from our mortal sight. We would
feel how little we know, how short-sighted is our vision.
We would know how much there is of purity that we have
never felt, how much of justice we have never seen, of
sweetness we have never known, of hope and expectation
that we have never cherished. We would believe, in our
life, that there are worlds on worlds of knowledge, of wisdom, of good, of sanctity, of loving kindness, and good
will, which eye hath not seen, nor ear heard, nor the

---

* "The Religion of Humanity." An Essay. (In Twelve Discourses.) By Octavius B. Frothingham. Third Edition. New
York : George P. Putnam's Sons.

heart of man comprehended. We would believe that these worlds are round about us all the time. We would believe that, whatever we may have of faith or hope, of love or earnest desire, we can enter into and bring down into our hearts the peace and strength of these blessings. We would remember the character of those before us, the gifts that have come down to us, the light of glory in our darkness, of hope in our fears, of courage in our weakness, of faith in our doubt, of peace and joy in our sadness and sorrow. In a world so full as this of doubting and questioning; where there are so many things to be asked, and answers are so few; where the problems are so deep and perplexing, and the solution of them so far away; where there is so much to be borne and forborne, so much to be remembered, and so much to be forgotten; where there are so many debts to be forgiven, so many evils to be eradicated, so many wounds to be healed, and so many patients to be cured; where there is this perpetual struggle; where we must lift ourselves up by such strength as we possess—we would remember the great words of faith and courage that echo through all the ages, responded to by the earnest hearts of mankind, the strong-hearted men, the noble, sainted women, who, with hearts full of affection, and souls bright with glory, and minds thirsting for truth, have walked their short journey in life, and done the work given them to do while the day lasted, and, in parting, have left behind them contributions to the world of human activity and human nature.

And we would be profoundly grateful for all these aids,

and supports, and benedictions, and by our endeavor we would make them not less, but more ; richer, not poorer ; to help ourselves and to help our fellow men to renew their lives, and so render praise and glory forever to the Author of Supreme Goodness and Life.

This prayer, equally with George Eliot's noble lines beginning, " Oh, may I join the choir invisible," breathes the spirit of reverence for the saints and martyrs of humanity; but does not aspire to the utter self-abnegation implied in her relinquishment of the desire for a personal immortality beyond the grave.

After another hymn, the sermon is delayed for a few moments, during the admission of a new multitude of late comers, who arrive for the purpose of listening to this unique discourse. An air of mutual acquaintance pervades the congregation, more noticeable than in other churches ; but there are many strangers, attracted by the reputation of the preacher, and disposed to be sharply critical of what they are to hear.

The Sermon.   Judged simply as an intellectual performance, the sermon is almost without a modern counterpart. However impressive the genius, fervor, oratory, of the most noted preachers belonging to our established sects, there is no one of them whose spirit is more eloquent and imaginative, and no one who relies so utterly upon the force of reason in his teachings, or who ventures to proffer his audience a discourse so thoroughly demanding attention and the exercise of the mental powers. While profoundly reverential, he reverses the method of evangelical preachers, and essays to reach the heart through the brain—through the perceptive, reasoning, and æsthetic faculties. He prefers to take the hearer in his sanest, acutest mood—his most logical mood; in the full possession of the judgment with which a human being is endowed.

As he stands with his sinewy but light and graceful figure, apart from the desk, you see that, although

Method and characteristics.

his discourse may have been carefully prepared, it is to be spoken, not read; you realize that it cannot have been literally memorized, and you study the play of his features as he begins, without flaw or impediment, to speak and " think while on his feet." It is a remarkable piece of intellectual oratory, exciting the surprise of cultured listeners. Commencing without a text, but with the announcement of a theme, he continues for an hour or more to pour out a stream of thoughts in language nearly as compact as Emerson's prose, yet so clear that even his youngest auditors are persuaded by its charm. We should compare his thought to Emerson's for closeness and wisdom, but it is arranged upon a logical system which is absent from the epigrammatic essays of the Concord sage. Frothingham's method is synthetic; he pays regard to the framework and order of his discourse. At times his expressions are highly poetical, and he warms into eloquence of looks, speech, and gesture. What the teachers call elocution is against him; his voice, in spite of himself, plays him tricks, and occasionally a word is inaudible at the close of a sentence. But he is all imbued with his theme, forces hearers to keep pace with him, and holds them to the end. Every face is directed toward him; young and old hang upon his lips, as if anxious that no word "should be lost." In the total absence of ordinary platform tricks this is, I

Triumph of
Pure Reason.
say, a triumph of pure reason. At the

close, even if you feel that you have been subjected to a certain mental tension, you acknowledge that nothing can be more fascinating than the study of so fine and free an intellect thus brought into play. There is no mental impoverishment; the audience departs well fed, and the food carries its own aid to digestion.

III.

What is the religion taught by this preacher, and how is this congregation, with its original forms of worship, gathered and sustained by his ministrations? Recalling the series of discourses preached at the Masonic Temple last winter, and condensing their essential matter, we may obtain a partial answer to these questions; availing ourselves, when practicable, of Mr. Frothingham's own words.

The Rational
Faith.
His rational or " reasonable " religion

is to be distinguished, first, from a religion founded, like Romanism, on authority; secondly, from a religion founded on simple faith. It claims to have reached a higher level than that of the Old or New Testament. It subjects the chronology, history, miracles of the Bible to investigation, and judges it to be a compilation, and not a single work divinely organized and inspired. It has no sealed book. Its canon of Scripture is not completed, nor will be. It reads all Bibles, Indian, Persian, or Christian. It opposes alike that " evangelicalism " which requires us to accept as revelation a special theory of the universe, and, on the other hand, that bald intellectualism which is equally intolerant in an opposite way. In distinc- tion from Calvinism, it believes that man's nature is radically good and only evil incidentally; were this otherwise, the human race would make no progress in morals and enlightenment. It recognizes the heart and soul of man, with his instincts and hopes. Finally, it discerns a perpetual revelation in the phases of nature, as elucidated by science. It has no fear of the term infidelity, as opposed to ortho- doxy, but regards the infidels of all periods as earnest and conscientious men ; often martyrs and pioneers of new thought. Infidelity is a great word and describes a great thing. It has been applied to holders of widely different opinions; to the primitive Christians, to the Jews of the middle ages, to the Protestants of the twelfth and thirteenth centuries, to historians, to the New England transcendentalists, to the school of Parker. It is used to describe the opinions of the minority, the suspected and hated few. Modern infidelity is of two kinds: the old, destructive school of Paine and the French revolutionists; the new, constructive religion which liberalists are professing. This religion is more than any particular system of faith, and much greater than the forms and traditions of the past; in fact, it is always seeking grander and more beautiful forms, a surer vision, a more radiant hope.

Mr. Frothingham does not hold himelf quite in sympathy with the woman of the Eastern fable, who

Consequences to be recognized.

bore a torch in one hand and a bucket of water in the other, that with the one she might burn up heaven and with the other extinguish hell. On the contrary, while preaching that right should be done because it is right, he also justifies a system based on hopes and fears; on a wise recognition of *consequences.* These he deems the enactments of the universe, and thinks that according to their natures they produce the conditions which people have dramatized under the epithets of heaven and hell. To be sure these words, in their theological sense, are spoiled phraseology, and no longer believed in. But they have had their restraining uses, have acted as a police force in the regulation of human affairs, and their place must still be supplied by a wholesome regard for the good or evil consequences which inevitably wait upon the observance or violation of universal law.

In answer to the question propounded by the advocates of tradition and authority, Why go to
Need of a Religious service. church? he takes occasion to explain and justify his own forms of worship. He proffers his religion and exercises to those who find the standard orthodox ceremonies flat, stale, and unprofitable. The aim of his service is to stimulate the mind and move the feelings in the direction of ideal thought, goodness, and beauty; it

belongs to those agencies by which men are elevated and made pure. To these ends it legitimately employs: (1) Music. (2) Reading of Scriptures which contain the antique wisdom of the race; all "sacred" writings that utter the solemn convictions of their ages and peoples. (3) Prayer. There is no religion without this. But to prayer he restores the original meaning, the heart's desire for unattained good. It is hunger and thirst for divine things, not a means for propitiating higher powers or establishing private relations with a patron deity. The desire is its own satisfaction; the petition its own answer. Omit this aspiration, and the spiritual or finest intellectual feature of his service would depart. (4) The sermon. This is addressed not to the emotions, but to the understanding. He does not, like the Romish priest or Protestant divine, arrogate a special inspiration by virtue of ordination or consecration. He has no gospel of redemption, no sealed commission; he claims for his words no authority, and affects to possess no knowledge above other men. It is his

Its aim and methods.

The Preacher's themes.

province to discuss subjects which people **require to have** presented statedly, **for** the reason that secular life tends **to keep them out of** mind.   **These** are not **the Trinity, deity of** Christ, atonement, and **other traditional** themes; **rather the relations of** man **to** man, the hopes and capacities of **the** race, the **significance** of the ancient words, God, immortality, life, death, **of worship, piety,** brotherly love.   **All** these he would interpret and illuminate **as matters** of **vital concernment, and apply their lessons to** the needs of **the hour.   In this way the higher** ministry **is attained, and** made **progressive and** perpetual.

Mr. **Frothingham's** views concerning the nature **and existence of** a Divine Being are frankly set forth

The Supreme Being. in three discourses,* remarkable for strength and beauty of expression, **entitled** " The Living God," " Thoughts About God," **and** " The **Theist's Faith."** His position relative to this subject **and to** the question of immortality,

---

* " Beliefs of the **Unbelievers, and Other Discourses."** By O. B. Frothingham.   New York : **G. P. Putnam's** Sons.

the two vital matters with every inquiring soul, has been so often scrutinized that he seems at pains to define it for the satisfaction of his hearers, and for his own vindication before the outer world.

He may be termed a theist, in the broad and aspiring sense of that word. Our thoughts of God, he says, are all that we have; but the picture framed by human mind is inadequate, whether that of the Trinitarian, the Unitarian, the Theist, or the Pantheist. Anthropomorphism is totally absent from his conception, and he discovers this quality in all religions of all races—from the savage to the modern Christian — in the faiths of the

Limitations of Human Thought. Indian, the Hebrew, the Greek, the Goth, the bigot, and the philosopher. To limit the Divine Being by our thoughts of him is fatal to humility, establishes dogma, perpetuates fable and tradition, makes Deity responsible for what is due simply to the limitations of our own minds. Human thoughts about God harden into tyrannous theologies. We arraign Providence by our own standards, not seeing that inflexible and eternal Law is the universal and benignant Providence;

we measure God **by our own** narrow **comprehen-sion**, **as if we could embrace** the vast **design.**
Therefore Frothingham foregoes all attempts to
conceive of a personal God. But let us quote his
own words :

In this it is not implied that God does not exist as **a**
being, but only that **we do** not apprehend him as **a** being. It is impossible **for me** not to believe that the universe
is governed **by an** intelligent will ; but **it is** equally impossible for **me to** imagine the nature of **the intelligence, or to**
conjecture the movements of the **will. Believe in the**
Supreme Power, **trust** it, repose **on it as we may, it still is**
a reality beyond our comprehension **or our reach.** This
is a point that **cannot** be seized **too firmly. The** stronger
my **faith in God the more modest my estimate of such** an
idea **of him as it is practicable** for me **to form.** The no-
tion that he might be such a being as mind **can conceive,**
no greater, no wiser, no nobler, would **drive me into** atheism. It is only by remembering faithfully **the utter** inad-
equacy **of** my thought that I can make **him** an object **of**
adoration.

With the sorrowful atheism of Mill, for **example,**
Frothingham **is wholly at issue.** He finds **peace**
The Reign of Law. and **satisfaction** in the **reign of** law.
He recognizes what **we call evil** as a
portion of a universal **plan** beyond **our** present

2

comprehension or arraignment, and believes in
God as "a power outside of us that works for
righteousness."* If this be so, the heart of the
theist is content. Faith in such a power, based on
what we can discover of the nature of things and
of the doctrine of development, is such a faith as
one may reasonably cling to.

He consequently does not seek to recall a van-
ished God, deeming a God who appeared and then
Conception of a Living God. disappeared to be more hopelessly absent than a God who never appeared.
Nor need we imagine a time when God will mani-

---

* From another prayer, taken from the report of the service at
Masonic Temple, June 4, 1876, we quote the following passage, in
further illustration of Mr. Frothingham's conception of the Supreme
Being :

"Spirit of Truth, Inspirer, Helper, Consoler, we invoke Thy
presence ; we implore Thy peace. Thou hast no name by which
we can call Thee ; Thou hast no form under which we can apprehend Thee ; Thou dwellest in no place ; Thou hast no temple ;
Thou speakest to us in no voice ; we have no thought that can com-
prehend Thee, no feeling that can do justice to Thee ; and yet we
may have Thee in our hearts ; through the dark paths of our life
we may be guided by Thee as our light. . . . We would feel
the privilege of being emancipated ever so little from the bondage
of prejudice and tradition, of being able to lift up our minds ever so

fest himself, nor solve the difficulty **with those**
revivalists who import a deity for **the hour.**

The **real question is,** whether **or no this** supreme
power—define **it and speculate about it as we will**—think
of it and reason about it as we may—is or is not LIVING—
a *real power* of intelligence and will, or nothing at all **but**
a fiction of our minds.   .   .   .   The universe is conceded,
by earnest, believing, religious men, not materialists or
skeptics, to be not so much a complicated machine, which
once made need not even be superintended, as a living
abode and ever-present manifestation of whatever being,
spirit, power it is that men call by the **name of deity.** . . .
So far then, the conception of a living God **is** made
definite.   No hint, **it may be, is** thrown out in regard to
the nature of infinite **being ; we are as** far, perhaps, as ever
from a knowledge of what God **may** be in 'himself ; nay,
the mystery of that may possibly be deepened ; still that

---

little above the clouds and tumults of the present to the serene and
everlasting light that is changeless and shadowless, forever and
ever.   We mourn not that what has been called inspiration has
ceased ; that great words **once devoutly listened** for are hushed : **that**
much that has been mistermed **knowledge has** passed away ; **that**
revelations which men have **waited for,** and longed for, and greeted
with uplifted **souls,** have lost their meaning for us.   We rejoice that
our hearts **are stirred** as with a divine **hope,** that **our minds** are
quickened with a deep and earnest love of knowledge, that **our** souls
are alight with glorious anticipations of human **good, that our** conscience has felt the power of unutterable **law, and** our. hearts the
sweetness of an unspeakable peace."

whatever power there is is alive, in every atom of space, in every instant of time, is put beyond controversy, and manifest, let us add, in a much higher form in mind than in visible matter.

It is then the object of the teacher's discourses, so far as theology is concerned, to seek for the *present* manifestation of this Supreme Being, discarding all other revelations, and to constantly obtain loftier views of His goodness and power.

Upon the question of immortality—*i. e.*, of the future existence of the soul in its separate individuality, preserving its affections, conscience, acquirements, memories, hopes, tastes, and perceptions—upon this question Frothingham's position seems not unlike Emerson's, to wit : that this " secret is very cunningly hid." He has referred to the belief of the early Christians in the resurrection of all who belong to Christ, and to the new doctrine of Dodwell and Clarke, the Oxford lecturers, who made the immortality of the soul a consequent upon its immateriality; but he finds no proof of all this, not even in the modern phenomena of "spiritualism." Yet in these and

The question of
Immortality.

other religious faiths he **discerns a " great hope,"** a

A Great Hope. hope **wide, encouraging, and sweet to men. To be permitted thus to** hope is **enough. The** mystery **of the future is its** charm. **The** hope of immortality is deeper and more universal than the belief **in it. It** seems never to die; it revives and **increases as the** faith in conscious continuance **in another state of** being declines. **Among** just **grounds for this hope he includes the** imperative **demand for justice, in view of the** apparent **disarrangement and incompleteness of** human **affairs; the incompleteness and** arrested development **of life and of the soul itself;** the starvation **and frustration of** our holiest natural affections and aspirations. **Reason lends** its ear to **such** cries, and those who **disbelieve in** creeds and revelation may well **cling to this magnificent hope.***

As to **faith itself, when** assuming the guise **of authority,** claiming **to hold the key to happiness**

---

* The question **of immortality is specially discussed, also, in** his sermon entitled **"'The Glorified Man," delivered April 16,** 1876. **(G. P. Putnam's Sons.)**

after death, and to possess a monopoly of **the**
privilege of admitting souls to it, he es-
teems this a sheer perversion of power.

Faith.

The pretension is that of supposition, not of faith.
Religion has no sympathy with it; true
religion strives **to** disengage itself from
this despotism, of which extreme types are found
in the iron sway of the Roman Catholic Church
and in the unyielding dogmas of the Calvinists.

It must rest up-on Knowledge and Aspiration;

But **faith** based upon knowledge **and**
upon loftiness of motive is a part of true
religion. The trouble is that it often claims to rest
on knowledge when it rests on fancy; to rest on
fact and its fact is fiction; to rest upon history,
and its history is mythology. The place
and work of true faith are admitted by
science itself:

Not upon Tra-dition and Authority.

Science.

For the scientific man lives by faith, in this sense : Faith
in the integrity of Nature, the omnipresence and inviola-
bility of law, the equivalence of forces ; faith that "the
universe was made at one cast," that mechanics and
mathematics are the same in all worlds, that sand grains
and planets obey the same kind of impulse ; faith of a
truly audacious and somewhat speculative sort.

Finally, a lofty and rational faith is the ground of moral enthusiasm and of every historic reform. The strong workers, the wise prophets, the bold achievers, have been men who believed in inviolable laws and principles, have been eminently men of faith.

IV.

Let us now consider this preacher's relations with the flock under his charge, and the nature of his practical admonitions. Teaching a rational not an authoritative religion, and always seeking new light for faith and hope, he naturally pays careful, learned, and eloquent attention to scientific discovery and social progress, and finds the clearest revelation of Deity in Nature's elements and processes, and the best evidence of " pure religion and undefiled" in the sympathy of man with man. His illustrations and arguments are largely drawn from scientific truths, of which no one is a more ardent and well-informed observer. His moral injunctions are pointed and incessant. He

The New Religion applied.

"More Light."

Morals vs. sentiment.

is a stern rebuker of the false and honeyed sentiment which tempts so many to venture upon dan-
gerous ground.   There is no sentimental looseness
or license in his doctrine.   Morals are of the first
importance.   Works, despised by the Calvinist, receive honor at his hands.   Spirituality
Good Works.
begins, continues, and culminates in use.
To be nobly, humanely useful is to be spiritual in
a grand way.   Love your neighbor more than yourself; pay your debts; lead pure and rational lives;
conform to the laws of nature; be honest even in
your secret heart.   After all these he fearlessly and
honestly endeavors.   He strives in every way to
nourish a close and delightful social
Social Brother-
hood.
brotherhood among his people.   As to
the worship of children, he enjoins upon parents
the duty of keeping the youthful heart untram-
meled either by selfishness or superstitious fear.

He finds in the very clogs of life its greatest
opportunities.   Even the clog of theology, the
stumbling-block of bigotry, the barricade
Evolution.
of dogmatism, have a use and value.
False religions have educated the human mind in

faith and courage, where sweet beliefs **would have**

Uses of Past   **failed.   The theology of New England,**
Error.

against which liberalism is a protest,

explains New England's moral growth:

Hard, acrid, angular, how many tender bosoms have
been bruised against it ; how many delicate consciences
and sensitive souls have been wounded and struck to death
by its sharp points !   And yet what a discipline in thought
it was !   For, when men were hedged round as with a line
of fire by these tremendous dogmas of predestination, de-
pravity, atonement, hell, it was imperative that they should
resist and react.   Reaction in favor of rational liberty of
mind could not be prevented.   .   .   .   It was the conscientious effort of those pious, painful men to find out the
truth within the limits appointed to them ; to grapple with
the terrible questions which their age propounded, and to
answer them as they could.   People who are brought up
outside of the old theology, who were born into liberalism
without personal knowledge of the older faith, having no
problems thrown down before them, and, consequently,
being discharged from the duty of turning them over, are
tempted never to ask, and failing to ask, become loose,
flaccid, and indolent in their minds.   We have to conjure
up for them new questions, to bring forward new problems
that will take the place of the grim old provocatives their
fathers knew.

The following extract from a recent discourse, en-

2*

titled "The Spirit of the New Faith," is of special
interest, as **giving** a clear statement of the teacher's
faith and purpose.

What is the new faith? What is its peculiarity?
What is its intellectual ground? The new faith rests
frankly and composedly upon the doctrine of evolution;
not maintaining the doctrine in any dogmatic sense;
not pretending to define it with scientific accuracy; but
accepting it in its broad meaning and lofty significance;
planting itself upon it as the most probable account of the
world's existence. Instead of believing that the creative
power and wisdom interposes to carry out special plans,
and to impart special ideas to the race, it is persuaded that
from the very beginning—from the *veriest* beginning—
things have been working themselves gradually out into
intelligent forms, into beautiful shapes, into varied use,
loveliness, and power. It contends that the world of humanity began at the beginning and not at the end. It
therefore discards miracles, rejects everything like supernatural interposition, considers as obsolete the popular
theory of revelation. It has no inspired books distinguished in character and contents from the world's best lit-
eratures. It sets up no teachers and prophets as proclaim-
ing an infallible word. It expects no infallible word from
any quarter. It reads no book with absolute or entire
reverence such as no other literature can receive. It sees
the work of the supreme will and wisdom in the ordinary
texture of the world, hailing its vital presence as an influ-

ence working toward light, order, righteousness, goodness, perfection in individual man and in the social groupings of mankind which are called societies. Planting itself upon this idea, the spirit that animates it must be peculiarly its own. It cannot be narrow, dogmatical, or exclusive ; nor can it be negative, scornful, or contemptuous. It stands beyond the very last attainment in charity.

. . . Charity is the last step that has been taken in religion by any considerable number of people. It is considered by most as the final step, the ultimate goal of kindness. The spirit of charity is commended by Christians as being the most excellent—the supreme spirit. But charity is not brotherhood ; it is not fellowship or appreciation. Charity can be unjust in its pity. Pity indeed is its essence. It does not scorn, but it does compassionate, and compassion is but a gentler form of contempt. In being charitable, one must believe that he or she has the sole, complete truth ; he scarcely more than tolerates ; only, instead of the haughty pride of toleration, he manifests kindness, gentleness, and a sentimental forbearance that forbids the demonstration of ill will. Charitable people may be indifferent in a way that to the sensitive is extremely disagreeable, and may be felt as extremely insulting. Charity too is limited. The churchman's charity is limited to church people. The dogmatist's charity does not pass cordially beyond the membership of his own communion.

The new faith therefore rises beyond charity to appreciation. It has no contempt ; it has no toleration ; it has no active or passive indifference ; it has more than nega-

tive good will ; it has the warm sentiment of brotherhood.
It can turn to the most abject forms of faith, the forms
commonly regarded as superstition, and recognize their
importance, their timeliness, even their benignity in the
periods when they prevailed. It can do justice to their in-
tent, their purpose, their being, when faith alone discloses
it. It can interpret their significance to their own believers unaware of their spiritual sense. It has no language of disparagement for men like Mahomet, Confu-
cius, Zoroaster, Pythagoras, Socrates, or any other renowned
teacher, reformer, or saint. It has no words of scorn for
men like Voltaire, Thomas Paine, d'Holbach, Helvetius,
Bolingbroke, the so-called, the self-styled infidels or athe-
ists of their day. It takes these men at their best—takes
their systems by their positive elements, enters into their
state of mind, their purposes and wishes, interprets them
from the inside motives that actuated them, and holds
them to account for what they meant to do and be, pre-
senting them as objects of regard to the fellow creatures
whom they thought to serve. The new faith takes the old
faiths by one hand and the modern faiths by the other,
embraces all earnest people, and cordially says : Let us be
friends ; we are all working together, thinking, hoping,
feeling our way into the realms of truth, conspiring to further the welfare of mankind. The new faith, thus taking
every mode of thought at its best, not at its worst, can do
justice even to abhorrent opinions. It says to the atheist :
You deny the existence of God ; you take Deity out of
the Heavens, leaving none but natural and human forces

in the world ; very well, then put Deity into your hearts. You say there is no Creator of the Universe ; but there must be creative power somewhere ; be yourself a creator. Do your utmost to put the regenerating powers that are within you into the task of making the material and moral world what it should be. You ridicule the idea of a Divine Providence ; but somebody must provide ; be a providence yourself in your own place and after your own fashion—a human providence, watchful, careful, helpful, kind. Show humanity that man has the capacity in himself for supplying his own necessities ; logic compels you to this ; compels you to look up, not down; to rank yourself with the affirmers, not with the deniers ; with the builders, not with the destroyers ; with the worshippers, not the desecrators.

The new faith approaches the materialist in the same spirit. It says to him : Be consistent with your own creed, and fulfill its positive requirements. You say there is no spirit in man or out of him ; that matter is all in all. Very well, spiritualize matter by exalting all its capabilities. You are bound to develop all the potencies of organization ; it is incumbent upon you, as you maintain that there is no supernatural, superhuman world, to unfold the possibilities of this world. You are certain that there is no hereafter ; teach men to honor, love, glorify their existence. Teach them to believe in this life ; believe yourself that the next life is the nearest life, and the nearest life is the life of to-day ; show them that you understand the worth of the hours ; make this life eternal, by packing it full of purposes and deeds that never perish.

Men come forward and boldly profess a yet darker creed, the creed of the pessimist. They deliberately avow their conviction that the world they live in is the worst world possible. They believe less than the atheist does, who simply denies the existence of a supreme power. The pessimist holds the controlling power to be evil. He believes in no tendency to righteousness or beneficence, he looks neither upward nor forward, recognizes no power outside of the world or inside of it that works with a prevailing purpose toward order and harmony. The new faith takes the pessimist, too, at his word. "This is the worst possible world, you say; if you have the moral perception to discern that, the moral sensibility to feel it and complain of it, the moral earnestness to denounce it, the duty of trying to mend the world is laid upon you. Is the world full of ugliness, wickedness, error, and sin? See if you can find nothing else in it; set yourself diligently to pick out the grains of beauty and grace, that lie like gems amid the ashes; preserve all the saving qualities you can discover; add to them your own; be yourself a hopeful, brave man, bent on disproving the fact that you as well as the rest of the world are good for nothing, a bit of driftwood or a devil."

When faith shall stand upon a spirit as live, sweet, tender, and encouraging as this, at once all heretics will be disarmed. The wars between the churches will cease; sectarian hatred must be at an end; religionist will no longer clutch religionist by the throat and drag him down. All true seekers, believers, hopers, aspirers, workers, will be confessed by one body, one fellowship, one family, contending together zealously to bring in a new order of things. This is the spirit of the new faith. Toleration it looks upon as utterly unwarranted. Charity at its best is exceedingly imperfect. It will accept nothing else than cordial and full appreciation of every earnest endeavor that is made by any thinker or worker for humanity. That the new spirit does not yet manifest itself as it should do among the disciples of the new faith we freely concede, "and more's the pity;" and this is the reason, if reason be required, why the new faith has not before this gathered hundreds.

It is to little purpose that we have garnered these thoughts from the outgivings of Mr. Fro-

Constructive Spirit of the New Faith. thingham, if it does not now appear that he has a very definite creed of his own in the liberal religion, and that he belongs to the constructive rather than to the old destructive order of spiritual reformers. In calling upon those who are dissatisfied with traditional theology to come out openly in favor of the new religion, and thus join the ranks of the searchers after truth, he is earnest and plain-spoken. Clearness and faithfulness in conviction he deems especially important in a period of transition, and he pays a tribute to Proctor for honesty in disavowing an inherited creed because it was inconsistent with his scientific faith. He takes up and demolishes, one by one, the pleas of the temporizer. You cannot place new wine in old bottles, and he that is not with the truth is against it.

Frothingaam, as we already have intimated, differs from other radicals by his comprehensive A judicial cast mental scope and impartial attitude. of mind. He certainly has little of the bigotry of reform, or of the pride that apes humility. Often his congregation is startled by some ground·taken which is precisely the opposite of what the more radical expect from him. Thus, in speaking of the Pharisees, he perceives their spirit among both the Philistine and Bohemian classes of all times; among conservatives and radicals, rich and poor, the formal and the free. It is the spirit which brings men of any class to set themselves apart as being worthier than their enemies or neighbors. This is the soul of Phariseeism, the source of exclusiveness, assumption, arrogance, and, of course, of bitterness, formalism, hypocrisy. There are

Pharisees philosophical, scientific, aristocratic, democratic, professional, orthodox, heterodox. The attitude of actors toward the clergy is nearly as pharisaical as that of the clergy toward the dramatic calling. The Bohemian may be a Pharisee as lofty in pretension as the Conventionalist, etc., etc. The strictly judicial cast of mind which prompts these utterances leads one often to think him unduly fond of paradox, until it is seen that what seems startling to others is to him the first and most truthful view of his subject. As his point becomes fairly understood, you perceive that he is an intellectual discoverer, with a method original and peculiar. Yet with all his reasoning, it has been well said that his " mind is log-

Style.

ical in its method of thought, but not in form of expression." The latter is often rhetorical, and seems discursive from its wealth of imagery and illustration. It should be remembered that he is speaking from the orator's platform, and that the printing of his discourse, as Ben Jonson said of written English, " is but an accident." He is a poet—one who masters and is not carried away by his imagination.   The æsthetic side of his nature

Taste and Cul-
ture.
is cultured to a rare and sensitive degree.
Taste is apparent in word, thought, action; yet he has rendered it subordinate to his duty as a teacher, and is not like him who

> ....built his soul a lordly pleasure house
> Wherein at ease for aye to dwell.

His predilections for art and literature are manifestly strong, and if he had followed authorship exclusively, he would be most distinguished in that calling.   His scholarship excels that of many learned doctors. If not elaborate in special fields, it is broad, rich, universal, covering with ardent and impartial view the literature of all peoples and times.

Owing to the popular knowledge of Mr. Frothingham's liberality toward all who desire to wor-

Personal quali-
ties.
ship after the dictates of their own natures, all sorts of new-fangled reformers and doctrinaires appeal to him and to his society for recognition or aid. If he has a weakness it is an excessive good nature, which makes him averse to utterly repelling even the most indiscreet.   His

charity in this respect often has led to a mis-
conception of his own views on the part of the
orthodox world, who father upon him many a
movement of which he may respect the aspiration,
and be heartily amused at the poverty or foolish-
ness of the creed. In reality the critical bent of
his mind has been so increased by training that,
as becomes an investigator, he subjects every fact
and doctrine to the most relentless scrutiny. A
disdain of empty sentiment never leaves him;
there is no obtaining emotions under false pre-
tenses at Masonic Hall. Conscience and sincerity
make him strong and clear. One who listens to
him for the first time might accuse him of lacking
that indefinable quality termed magnetism. But
he is in truth both magnetic and humane, full of
practical charities, and exquisitely sensitive to the
friendship of those whom he respects and loves.
In private life he is delightful, and, by his sweetness, humor, conversational tact, and power, the
inciter of general delight. To see him in his
home is a privilege indeed. Here, and among the
groups of his select acquaintance, he is the flower

of courtesy and companionship—a gentleman of the most refined and genuine school.

A word in relation to his published writings. "The Religion of Humanity," mentioned here-

Publications.
tofore, is a series of essays upon Modern Tendencies, God, the Bible, the Power of Moral Inspiration, Providence, Immortality, Conscience, the Soul of Truth in Error, and that of Good in Evil. Another of his volumes is "Beliefs of the Unbelievers, and other Discourses." His "Life of Theodore Parker " is an inspiriting and well-proportioned biography. It has been aptly succeeded by the " History of Transcendentalism in New England," a book which those interested in that remarkable phase and movement long ago called upon him to write ; and no other man, Dr. Ripley possibly excepted, is so fitted for the task, or could have accomplished it so readily and well. It is, in its way, a handbook of philosophic inquiry, from the time of Kant, and, as a record of New England transcendentalism and of the lives of the poetic, original beings who were the leaders of that movement, is, and will remain, an

indispensable authority. Mr. Frothingham always
has taken special interest in the ways, thoughts,
and culture of the young. Years ago he made an
attractive paraphrase of some familiar Scripture
legends, in two volumes, " Stories from the Lips of
the Teacher " and " Stories of the Patriarchs."
His " Child's Book of Religion," for Sunday schools
and homes, is a unique and attractive compilation,
prose and verse, for the enjoyment and religious
training of children. He has been a frequent
contributor to our leading magazines and reviews.
A feature of his church is the gratuitous distri-
bution of his more impressive discourses, steno-
graphically reported from week to week. These,
and all of his printed works, are issued and for sale
by the Putnams, and form a library of original
and eloquent religious teaching.

V.

Mr. Frothingham was born in Boston, and is now

Biographical.

at his prime, something more than fifty
years of age, although his face and figure
are those of a younger man. He belonged to the

Harvard class of 1843, went through the course of study at the Divinity School, and became, like his distinguished father, a Unitarian clergyman. For some years he was the pastor of a church in old Salem, but finally, after a period of study, controversy, and foreign travel, grew too radical and progressive to be bound by the ties of any existing organization. In 1855 he began to preach upon an independent basis to a small congrega- . tion in Jersey City. In 1859 he removed to New York, organized a society, and for some years preached in a church near Sixth Avenue, on Fortieth Street. After a time it was thought advisable to sell that building, and the society removed to Lyric Hall, which became famous through the reputation of its preacher. A peculiar congregation, though until recently a small one, gathered around him ; a fit audience, though few, making up in character and influence whatever it lacked in numbers and worldly wealth.

Mr. Frothing-
ham's " Soci-
ety."   Some of our choicest and best-known writers, thinkers, and philanthropists, have belonged to this society. It has also been

remarked that many thoughtful people, **long**
unaccustomed **to church-going, have** resorted to
Mr. Frothingham's church as to **a** place where
absolute freedom of conscience is proffered to
the worshipper.   No doubt it is looked upon
as **a** cave of Adullam by the orthodox; certainly it is the haunt of eager, restless, unsatisfied
spirits, attracted by the originality and boldness
of the preacher's views.   Members of the literary,
artistic, and dramatic guilds favor it, and here
you find a select group from the scholarly **and**
learned professions.   Many Israelites, of the **pro-**
gressive school, are scattered among the audience.
In the fall of 1875 the society removed from
Lyric Hall to its more convenient and beautiful
quarters in the Masonic Temple.   An immediate
and great enlargement of the congregation was
the result.   It has nearly doubled its numbers
and resources, **and the** hall, during the winter of
1875-76, was crowded with audiences listening to
a brilliant and notable series of discourses.   Marked
attention was given to this series by that portion
of the press which is on the alert for what is

most significant among the men and matters of
our time.

The spirit of the society is declared by the
"rules" of the "Independent Liberal Church"

The Indepen- to be not in any sense ecclesiastical
dent Liberal
Church. or dogmatical, but purely social. No
distinction is allowed between members of the
"church" and members of the "congregation."
The society is "cordial, open, humane; its welcome is warm, its sympathies are wide, and it relies
on these qualities for its influence and success."
But one regular service with preaching is held during the week, that of Sunday morning, the after-
noon of Sunday being devoted to pastoral lectures
and instruction. Social reunions occur on secular
evenings, at intervals, and are of a pleasant and
entertaining nature. A peculiar feeling of brotherhood exists among the frequenters of the church.
No sacraments are observed or rites adminis-
tered. The ceremony of christening, or the dedi-
cation of childhood, as a social rite of poetic significance, is performed by the pastor when requested.
The association was originally incorporated in

1860, under the title " Third Congregational Unitarian Church." This title has been changed,
and for some years past the church has openly
maintained an unsectarian position. This is in ac-
cordance with the principle announced in its con-
stitution, which declares that it is " established for
the support of public worship, the maintenance of
a religious faith, liberal, intelligent, and progressive, the cultivation of religious life, individual and
social, insisting always on freedom of individual
opinion in all matters of religious belief, and claiming to be responsible only to God and the private
conscience." A section of the by-laws declares,
" It is expressly understood that no subscription or
assent to any covenant or formula of faith shall be
required of any member."

The national " Free Religious Association " is
an organization which counts upon the list of its
directors such names as Emerson, You-
mans, Curtis, Higginson, Weiss, Sar-
gent, Lucretia Mott, Lydia Maria Child. Frothingham's position as the most active and eminent
leader, since the death of Parker, of the liberal

The Free Relig-
ious Associa-
tion.

movement in America, is confirmed by the
action of this body. At the time of its forma-
tion he was unanimously elected to the presiden-
cy, an office which he still retains. His own
church, as we have seen, has reached a vigorous maturity. Leaving out of question the vitality
claimed for such an institution as we have de-
scribed, it is exposed to perilous contingencies, being held together and nurtured by the force of a
master who as yet has but few professional asso-
ciates, and to whose place no one at this moment
could fitly succeed.

—————

Our sketch, however inadequate, of a remarkable teacher, his system, and the church under his
guidance, must now be ended. But even this much
will serve to show that many notions current with
respect to Octavius Brooks Frothingham are utterly superficial; that his reverential and judicial
qualities are on a level with his acknowledged intellectual genius, and that he exerts in this community, and throughout the world of religious aspiration, a constant, earnest, and most potential force.

BOOKS BY OCTAVIUS B. FROTHINGHAM.

THE RELIGION OF HUMANITY. An Essay.

Third Edition—Revised. Price, $1.50.

"Nobody can peruse this book without respect for the learning, mental honesty and skill in the statement of his convictions, possessed by the author, and for the essential integrity and philanthropic tendency of his spirit."—*Springfield Republican.*

"A profoundly sincere book, the work of one who has read largely, studied thoroughly, reflected patiently. * * * It is a model of scholarly culture and of finished and vigorous style."—*Boston Globe.*

"A marked book, forming a most important contribution to our religious literature."—*Boston Register.*

THE CHILD'S BOOK OF RELIGION.

For Sunday-Schools and Homes. Price, $1.00.

THE SAFEST CREED, and other Discourses.

12mo, Cloth, $1.50.

We commend these discourses, not "as food for babes," but as full of suggestion for earnest and thoughtful men.

STORIES FROM THE LIPS OF THE TEACHER.

With Frontispiece. Cloth, $1.00.

"The Parables are so re-told as to absorb the attention of the reader, and to fasten upon the mind what the writer believes to have been the impression the Saviour meant to convey. It is in style and thought a superior book, and will interest alike young and old."—*Zion's Herald* (Methodist.)

STORIES OF THE PATRIARCHS.

With Frontispiece. Cloth, $1.00.

"A work of culture and taste : it will be welcome to all ages, and gives the sublimest lessons of manhood in the simple language of a child."—*Springfield Republican.*

BELIEFS OF THE UNBELIEVERS. A Lecture.

12mo, Paper, 25 cents.

TRANSCENDENTALISM IN NEW ENGLAND. A History.

With sketches and studies of Emerson, Alcott, Parker, Margaret Fuller, the Brook-Farm Community, etc.

8vo, Cloth extra, with steel portrait of the author, $2.50.

THE LIFE OF THEODORE PARKER.

8vo. With Portrait, $3.00.

SERMONS

OF

O. B. FROTHINGHAM.

SECOND SERIES.

The above Sermons, and those remaining of the First Series, are for sale by the Publishers, or are sent by mail, paid, at the price of 10 cents each; and subscriptions are received for the Series for the year (planned to consist of 20 Sermons), at $2 each.

It has been decided to put upon the Sermons for the present merely such nominal price as is expected to meet the cost of their publication.

www.ingramcontent.com/pod-product-compliance
Lightning Source LLC
Chambersburg PA
CBHW031802090426
42739CB00008B/1120